SMOKES

SMOKES

Susan Wheeler

FOUR WAY BOOKS
Marshfield

Editorial Office
Four Way Books
PO Box 607
Marshfield, MA 02030

Library of Congress Catalog Card Number: 97- 61430

ISBN 1- 884800-19- X

Cover: Michael Corris Design
Text: Acme Art, Inc.

This book is manufactured in the United States of America and printed on acid- free paper.

Four Way Books is a division of Friends of Writers Inc., a Vermont-based not-for-profit organization. We are grateful for the assistance we receive from individual donors and private foundations.

Also by Susan Wheeler

Bag 'o' Diamonds, University of Georgia Press, 1993

Acknowledgments

American Letters and Commentary: "Carnivorous Fowl, and Otherwise," "Fractured Fairy Tale"

B City: "Run on a Warehouse" section II

Bomb: "Two Regrets," "White Exiles"

chain: "The Blanching Heart"

Chelsea: "Instructions," "Invective: You Should Know"

Colorado Review: "The Dogwood and the The," "The Lip of the Snow in Lapland," "Ezra's Lament," "Clock Radio," "Chosen"

Columbia: "Oldest Psalter"

Denver Quarterly: "Smokes"

Nedge: "Rehearsal for *The Breaks*"

New American Writing: "The Homewrecker (in 7/4)"

The New Yorker: "Shanked on the Red Bed"

The Paris Review: "Alphabet's End," "Run on a Warehouse" section I, "Landscaping for Privacy," "Knit in Your Will"

Pequod: "He or She That's Got the Limb, That Holds Me Out on It," "Ethic," "Song for the Spirit of Natalie Going," "Meeting Again, After Heine"

Poetry International: "Casino Night," "Knot Me"

The Poetry Project Newsletter: "Possessive Case," "Sonnet of Alternate Starts for a Poem of Comparison," "The View from There"

St. Luke's Review: "Pantoum: His Dying"

Sugar Mule: "Molloy for Girls"

Western Humanities Review: "Beavis' Day Off," "Sap Assured: on the Set"

Witness: "Framingham," the final section of "White Exiles"

"Ezra's Lament" also appeared in *Ecstatic Occasions, Expedient Forms* (Macmillan, 1996), and "Run on a Warehouse" in *The Best American Poetry* (Scribner, 1996).

The author acknowledges the assistance of the New York Foundation for the Arts and Lynchburg College in the writing of these poems, and is grateful to David Jacobson, David Trinidad, Lawrence Joseph, Julia Kasdorf, Michael Tyrell, Sarah de Bienville and, ever and always, to her husband Philip.

for Jodi Sisk and for Daniel Harding Wheeler
truest siblings

Contents

I

II

III

I

ergo corporeum uocem constare necessest,
multa loquens quoniam amittit de corpore partem.
T. Lucreti Cari, *De Rerum Natura*, IV.540-541

Speech, then, is matter; this we must admit,
Since he who speaks at length loses some weight.
Lucretius, from *The Nature of Things*, IV.540-541
tr. Frank O. Copley

He or She That's Got the Limb, That Holds Me Out on It

The girls are drifting in their ponytails
and their pig iron boat. So much for Sunday.
The dodo birds are making a racket
to beat the band. You could have come too.

The girls wave and throw their garters
from their pig iron boat. Why is this charming?
Where they were nailed on their knees
the garters all rip. You were expected.

The youngest sees a Fury in a Sentra
in a cloud. This is her intimation and she balks.
The boat begins rocking from the scourge
of the sunset. The youngest starts the song.

Rehearsal for *The Breaks*

I

He was WHACKED with religion.
And he was trying yea so mightily
not to sound spoon-fed, he,
a cynical man,
educated to 30.

I GOT no ongoing circumstances.
He sinks upon the velvet seat
and codes the program back
in fribbling s'rrows.
A burning fire shut up in my bones—

II

After a sort of amiable striding-about the posy-snippers stop at the edge of the audience and doff their shoes. They are not sure what makes the crowd so high-strung and fickle tonight. They are too far back to see the gameboard and point-of-play.

III

No no no, THAT Francis Bacon.
Is this his own voice, this
twirling and trafficked, gnarly
thing? What in the end
would his mother have said

hearing dicta to rival her own,
dangling the glorious bag
empty of chips in the
crackled sun? She might have
thought him snoring.

IV

They've had it with the hamstrung one. It's at a tricky point, where
traditionally six glass marbles sweep the board and end up in
Welsh Rarebit sauce. (*She* prefers ketchup on Saltines, but
heat it. The marbles crack from hot to ice.)
The wiggly crowd near the wisteria inhales and holds its breath.
The shooters are cued for the poof-in, to begin pummelling like rain.

V

Instead of your going
horsewires you can just say
"Chia needed somethin'" awright?
Chia! Y'know – chia pet! What
gentleman there is within thy wire scratching—

That voice again. He could deep-six
the lot of 'em, that risible lead
in his floppy tam, the starlet whose
pudenda pendulums before Tab A inserts.
His addled nerves deliberate.

VI

This was the last word I was going to peel for you. You watch cars out
the window as you chew, and I try to explain before you're through
where last I saw the vocabulary. Stage left, before the mongering crew
gave the multitudinous audience a shoo and from then on out
it was cash & carry. No one's interest got furthered today.

VII

It's grace that's given them this
smoker of a grand design,
this man so WHACKED he stokes
the script with rewrites palmed unto
the hapless stand-in scripter, she,

a mistrust of loquacity, a finger
flecked with 'raser threads, an
impedimented personality.
That was my plan for him, hubristically.
A reclamation of sorts, after sodden reprieve.

Beavis' Day Off

He'd been doing a lot of cull-twanging,
he thought, walking back and forth on the deck
of his battleship *whoa! correction:* loft.

Small fires burned on the outskirts of Soho;
Fanelli's lit up under a stickered sky:
cirrus pitched to the top of its firmament.

How long could he crimp the diesel in the dark?
The bedlam was breathing its own air now;
the parrot shivering in the freezer glared at the hen.

Please it's time said Meg. And each infernal
truism struck a package deal for tin.

What hast thou, O nut job, with paradise?
The sparks O they crested the floor then they floated
and she lay down on fine braids and she cried.

The Dogwood and the The

> "And in the center of the outer edge of each petal there
> will be nail prints, brown with rust and stained with
> red, and in the center of the flower will be a crown of
> thorns, and all who see it will remember. . . ."
>
> —from various postcards, "The Legend of the Dogwood"

The dazzling platters of the many-armed man,
The hundred plates spinning on the hundred spun fingers,
A trick whip *Step ON it you* soft in the skim of your skin—

The eye becomes inured to gaud. The bellicose kids fort up
The grand screen. *Cool, summa, wahm in the winta—*
Hey asshole! Take ya stringy hair out! The quarter's in,

The blip's on Calvary, the lamps of the memory palace under
Glass blink up at Ig. They were each a dipsy-doodle at heart
And the night washed in like ink. *Summer bun it drive me*

Crazy. And he said, *prosper beneath the blue water tank.*
And they said, *the fugger got it on hisself.* And I said,
Wait in the glen. A minute so I. Catch up wif you.

The tree don't know from passion. A stun gun blusts and
Blood scats in the glass, one player beating with his fist in time—
There has been a casualty. The bereaved will have their needs.

Exemplification Avenue

That was the great escape. I told you once.
They gathered the shanties and the garrisons
down near the lot where the Clydesdales come
until Lula herself could bake enough pies.
She said *I betcha a million bucks those ones*
then the rush of all wings took her too.

Steady, the ash that blows, the ailanthus pod
that odors garp, the ridge of beeches by the
interstate: a fragile wind is flailing you.

Norton, swinging back and forth beneath the
attic's peak, misses the telescope.
I found the mustard but not the bread.

Yeah, that was before he is leaning out,
from the car now, and tacking. He is
telling the tale of the serious times. We
cannot imagine the ways that they flinched then.
He cannot find words to imprint it on us.

Here. A child bends in to hear the crying.
The cart surmounts the astonished mall.

Pantoum: His Dying

There he is, on the pillow: the squirrel.
If it ain't broke, it ain't breakable.
Fort Howard and Stylene conspire to the dizzy
at the brink of the basin in the dark.

If it ain't broke, it ain't breakable.
The sorry squirrel's breathing riddles the ears
at the brink of the basin in the dark.
Give him the ice pop and uncrease the bedclothes.

The sorry squirrel's breathing riddles the ears
while a tumult of clattering darts in from out.
Give him the ice pop and uncrease the bedclothes
and prepare the ridiculous sacrament, gone.

While a tumult of clattering darts in from out,
Fort Howard and Stylene conspire to the dizzy
and prepare the ridiculous sacrament, gone.
There he is, on the pillow: the squirrel.

Ethic

Manman got a special s'rup 't cures the lonelies.
All the night, up the tree'f the pickling shed
Ise drinking from it elixir.

Afters the sunup the hacked meat it come.
The truck it seethes on it brakes and the driver he look
Ise swinging from t'friendly tree.

Then it smote. What business was mine
in the cardboard rune, in the native rap?
I on the tree stump, I missing all.

The Lip of the Snow in Lapland

The child pirouettes on the path to the igloo,
scoping its lights on the snow in the dark.

To each is given manifestation of the Spirit.

Lunch will be fish and the hot clotted soup
over Elvis tapes on the new soundbox.
Everyone else will be smoking Kents.

All these are activated by one and the same Spirit.
A glow on the lip of the snow means noon.

And the fractals experts, after summer
institutes, got on your husband's nerves.
Joey zipped the lawn bugnet and
settled in for the long exposé.

The child spins in a bright kitchen lamp
then she gums. *To another various kinds of tongues,*
to another the utterance of knowledge
according to the same Spirit.

The soup is hot in the dark of the day.

Smokes

for David Trinidad

At the Chelsea Hotel, you sat on the edge of the bed while he rummaged
through drawers for cigarettes. The wind set by a big tumult at the glass.
Scrafing the view, the lone plane tree scissored an arm and subsided.
Suppose he had at that moment put his hand on your arm and said *Ethan*.
You would have had to have told him this was not your name, that indeed
you know no Ethan, Ethan may be an actor but what writer was Ethan,
and hadn't he summoned you here? In Washington, they called them
redbuds, what was in bloom. Besides, suppose instead of correcting him
you had finally reached into your pocket for Luckys, had offered him a
Lucky, and his gratitude and relief were discernible in the slight gesture
he would make for you to wait while he found the poem. On the way in,
you had just seen a small girl in a flat halter jumping at you from the stair.
"Can you imagine planting redbuds in front of a brick house?" the Virginia
intellectual asked. Beyond the glass the light and the wind were becoming
Peter Brooks' storm scene from King Lear. Suppose then that he found the
sheet of paper that he was looking for and with Buddha's frown if Buddha
frowned he inhaled from the Lucky and the left corner of his lips rose as he
read over silently the poem, and then settled beside you on the bed taken
without giving any indication with your raven hair, your nervous laugh
Suppose then he said, *Ethan, here it is. To live! To live!* he would read,
watching you without seeming to. The forsythia bursts out first with the
first single-headed daffodils; they riot with fire. In Atlanta, these have
long come and gone by now. Suppose all of this happened, and this attention
was really there. Suppose he attended to the delicacy of your attention.
Suppose he was a good mom, suppose he didn't brush your arm with his arm.
The sky darkened so quickly that the plane tree appeared spooky.
A siren scrawled a wail down 23rd Street that made it impossible to speak,
in the room. You took this opportunity to light another Kool and
saw your hands shake although you were young. Suppose with the brush
of his arm it was difficult to follow the poem but it was a poem to die for,
all of the nouns lined up and fascinating. Suppose he said, *Ethan, what
do you think*? There was a time when johnny jump-ups preceded forsythia,

the good old days. Evolution was the driving force behind the leapfrogging.
Everyone had assumed you had meant something different than you did,
afterwards, when you gave your account of the room. You saw the spring
as though beyond a shutting door. The older poems—I mean by centuries—
have given us enough time to really love them. Suppose you had responded
with unmediated admiration. Suppose then: *So Ethan, where are yours*?
After you lit the Kool and the siren fell you heard over the racket of the wind
a child running outside the door. A ladyslipper in a Strohs bottle by the bed
made you think of Gloria Swanson in her last days, waxy and semi-trans-
lucent, speckled brown on green. He poured himself another Coke.

Suppose then that under the ginkgo on Mercer Street when the storm's
lid had latched he had said *Come with us Ethan why don't you?* The young
at the least can decorate. This would have been like the Santa Maria,
bumping the lap of the Easthampton pier, waiting its turn for a roll. Night
air whooshed the opaque, lit wall. You waited for this, and he didn't.
The redbud's a small tree, a scrapper, an adamant. Some are strong, some
weak, some like you with the breath of forgiveness cupping to light a Kool.

II

Ce temps où je vis, ce temps malhereusement s'écoule et m'entraîne. L'impatience folle, comme accidentelle, dans laquelle il se comprend, ne m'épargne pas.

André Breton, *Les Vases communicants*

The time I live in, this time, alas, runs by and takes me with it. The crazed and, as it were, accidental impatience in which it is caught up spares me nothing.

André Breton, *Communicating Vessels*
tr. Mary Ann Caws & Geoffrey T. Harris

Ezra's Lament

I owed the baker three dollies with heads.
I owed the singer a way to recoup.
I owed the bookmaker my mother's own sauce.
I owed the outfielder plenty, plenty.

I owed the swimmer a new way of speech.
Lucky I was that the view of the villa
Prevented my pitching the book overboard.
I owed the industrialist pinafore threads.

I owed the waters drops from my lenses,
I owed the bereaved, I owed a tiger,
A dentist, a hobbyist, a smallish crook,
The maîtresse d'hôtel—the shiniest stones.

What breath employs me thats salary should be
Paid in tenders I don't understand?
The bankruptcy makes ichnites of heirlooms
Strung across oxidized fiberboard pegs.

I owed Winslow a flowering grove, a bower.
I owed a simpleton plenty, plenty.
I owed the gentlest of Barbie collectors
A wracked afflicter and a soupçon of sand.

Machinate carefully, o if you should go there,
Clicking the debts like a rotary phone
Where the lifeline is sparked in the vectors.
That frantic believing will break you in two.

I owed who raised me the still of my back,
the television's glint in the model set store,
and I owed my brother a bike.
I owed the fence these colorform 'toons.

The parch in the Playland is criminogenic.
I owed the insects swarming the creditors
Their own salt hearts, brittling the trees.
The army, and air force, plenty I owed.

O if you should go there in your twenty years
Remember the wank that you cannot repay,
O if you should, there in your twenty years.

Alphabet's End

So I'll speak ill of the dead. A was crooked,
planting the small left finger of the raccoon in the upholstery
before he sold the car. B made certain to point out Celia's
bewildered look before her pink slip came in the flimsy institution.
In the videos of C, a jejune overwhelmed the cast.

D built dollhouses. Even Lonnie down at Shell
found him less a man for it, the night they went off to see the stock
cars break. I wanted E's hair, but by the end it was no more. F
refused alms, pulling the man up by his shirt in the street, and
G sought rewards. Marybeth said H fondled her for sport.

Now you, I, Smokey, hell
bent on a village version of Club 21, embarrassed by our attentions.
Mistrust it was. Dig me a chamber of preparedness.

William T. Osborn 1964–1993

Possessive Case

What are you walking the hamjammies for.
It's always the same argument. The man scrapes
the molt from his forearm and cringes.

The scabs become virulent in their saucer.
The man harnesses their latent energy.
The man continues to prick, pick at the girl.

Seven flight suits are pounding at the door.
Words pound from seven visors. The words
fall in the saucer and make a molten pot hash.

The marquee in the saucer draws waterbugs.
Their inelegant eyebrows make needles for the girl.
He *might* have been capable of love. Worth trying.

The giant engine with its pistons of lamb arms
glides down their street on its skis. The pilots
use their balcony for streamers. Cheers.

Scabrous wasn't such a big deal. Where's the oven?
Under the spreading oak tree a steel filament blew.
He puts his johnson in his pants and begins to stew.

Invective: You Should Know

One

Now you are in a lather over their taking the Scrabble pieces and using them for decoration. Refresh yourself, bone up on organizational skills, *a three-ring binder and this new version of Whist will fit you out like new*. For they are beginning to talk when you bend to tie your shoe. They say, *the 'x' goes perfectly in this xylophone*. Before the Roman with the brogue begins his hatcheting, you will have draped yourself as a workhorse courtesan with plenty of extra letters to spare. You will have blanks for everyone, on demand. They will know *just how invaluable you are: their burgeoning pockets will attest to it*. So now, wipe the spittle from your rouged chin. The players are waiting for you.

Two

I knew my hand was not a valued commodity since I could not bring a powerful or even compelling family to it. It started with your dad's sweater, *that wonderful Italian cut*, watching you carried away by the romance of your dancer dad. Well it wasn't just *your* romance, everyone it seemed had a way of embellishing a family or in-laws—except perhaps for the thoroughly jaundiced, like mom, who didn't like anyone but the chirpy and anxious "helpers." It started when you held out the sweater and said, *Here it's my father's, it's a wonderful Italian cut, you can borrow this*. Suddenly all the Vegas motifs to the apartment lent you, the bearer, a tragic kind of 20th century captive of sleaze giant kind of thing, dangling the Italian cut sweater from your outstretched arm.

Three

In the meeting room your chaps, Festus, seemed out of place. How sunnily you seem to find the filetab that attaches to each article in seven. There was some talk among us studio sausages that you had run aground on the Foreign Correspondence project and canned the rest, and that is why you hum to yourself at table. Yesterday I saw your wife picking peaches into your rival's basket—she had the softest smile, like strawberries, hellbent on your ruin.

Four

I hadn't forgotten the favor you had done me in the barn catercorner to the milkpond those some ten years ago, and when that peacenik spoke ill of you I rose to your defense. I told him about your cock, dear heart, about the wiggle in its walk and the soft cradle you made of the down for my head. If I mentioned the leg you ran off with, my only steed, if I happened to say that the books you were selling could not substitute, if I said that your fingers were as fast and my fall as great as Lucifer's, that you and I are much alike, that His Will it was and His Will is cruel, if the peacenik then stared with incredulity, well you will have heard it all before, no, my precious one?

Song for the Spirit of Natalie Going

Small bundle of bones, small bundle of fingers, of plumpness, of heart,
predicate, prescient, standing and wobbling, lit up in the joy,
lachrymose GA, your bundle oh KA, the unfolding begun of the start,
of the toys, of witnessing, silly, the eyes startled and up, re-
énveloped now and fresh with the art, chordate, devoted,
sunk in dreaming of wisps and startled awake—*This is morning.*
This is daddy. This is the number eight—spacey, resplendent,
in seersucker bib, overalled, astonished, in dazzling fix
on the small crawling lights in their spaceship of night and the
plug and the cord and the big one's delight, pausing,
mezzed by mobile HEH HEH and again, stinging the shopkeepers
the monkeyish mouth, *knees, child knees—need to have the child*
here—absence—knees fall—and falling, a dream, a final
singsong UH HAH in the starkest of suns, the heat now a blanket
now a song of your soul—Such a sharp love there is! Such a loud
love there beats! Such a filled hole you leave, in the dusk in the room,
in the wobbling hours of what has refúged, your future in me.

Natalie Joy Hertel-Voisine, 1994-1995

Sap Assured: On the Set

The attenuated sinew
Out on the back lot as
The sun comes up,
After too much coffee,
Fighting off crullers,
Keeping the random stars
In rigorous row,

Tugs at your gluteus
And grows. The randy,
Pixillated prince
Berates the fairy's con-
Comitant disregard;
Entrailered by the Benz
The sheik fights off

The hiccups now; a
Dancing mouse, all but
Disappeared, scatters
Through the soap flakes.
The night tips up at
Last its roof and salts
Your bath with lucre.

Shanked on the Red Bed

The perch was on the roof, and the puck was in the air.
The diffident were driving, and the daunted didn't care.
When I came out to search for you the lauded hit the breeze
On detonated packages the bard had built to please.

The century was breaking and the blame was on default,
The smallest mammal redolent of what was in the vault,
The screeches shrill, the ink-lines full of interbred regret—
When I walked out to look for you the toad had left his net.

The discourse flamed, the jurors sang, the lapdog strained its leash—
When I went forth to have you found the tenured took the beach
With dolloped hair and jangled nerves, without a jacking clue,
While all around the clacking sound of polished woodblocks blew.

When I went out to look for you the reductions had begun.
A demento took a shopgirl to a raisin dance for fun,
And f'r you, for me, for our quests ridiculous and chaste
The lead sky leered in every cloud its consummate distaste.

The mayors queued for mug shots while the banner rolled in wind
That beat at bolted windows and bore down upon the thin,
And everywhere warped deliverers got bellicose and brave,
When I walked out to find you in the reconstructed rave.

The envelopes were in the slots and paperweights were flung.
When I came down to seek you out the torrents had begun
To rip the pan from handle and horizons from their shore,
To rip around your heady heart looking there for more.

Carnivorous Fowl, and Otherwise

He was a braggart, and he wasted little time
in swaying everybody west of Miracle Mile
to his side. Anyway, the clam dogs weren't
anything to ~~right~~ write home about.

How those smokestacks are pumping! Eh? He
had just sliced into the new Jersey tomatoes
when she appeared, a vixen she. That highway
there will cut right through Mo's Ravine,

and hug the valley shoulder. Look at that
speckly mustard there! Flex and point!
Desiderata house on fire.

Weren't long before we'd sent that one
back up to Lonnie's Gulch, since there's no room
for bullies here. Anyway, she ate the plums,
the plums that I was saving, plums for you.

Instructions

Imagine you
beneath the flue
should ventilate
with zest too great
and proximate
a fire bait
without equip,
a nozzle, tip
and creosote spray
to save the day.

The whoosh of air
and ignition there
might shake you so
you'd have to throw
yourself upon
a rug or john
and roll or splash
the flames that lash,
then up and go
to the right window
for the fire escape
(you painters, scrape!),
open it and leave
so I not grieve.

For though you be
immortal, He
guards the few
in His purview
whose hubris pales
before they fail.

The Homewrecker (in 7/4)

The homewrecker fingers my watch
like an urn. Her wrist is glued
to the back of her head. Her fingers flap
in the onrushing of the Jeep Commandoes.

I haven't gotten it yet. She is patient
while I'm lining up the marbles in the bowl.
She is patient like lead. She waits with bare
impatience and then re-articulates the strophe.

When she offers me a drink I take it.
When she asks me a question I answer it.
When I answer it she is floored by my answer.
I think, *how little she knows me.* Again.

The interloper wears an apron to the movies
and uses the comrade handshake. My mouth
is open, I know. The cavities in my mouth
play harmonics, they do it without me.

Without me, she waits by the bed, she is poised.
Her patience insults. The bed corrodes
beside her, its posts beat like wings, the bedskirt
shrinks to puny of its own accord.

Perfume? Why care we. The gas man tests
ignition and presents his bill. My fill.

The Blanching Heart

> "From thy Bright Eyes he took his fire,
> Which round about, in sport he hurl'd;
> But 'twas from mine he took desire . . ."
> —Aphra Behn, "Song. Love Arm'd," 1684

The hero, such as he was, in the classroom,
in the evening, found the crosstalk taxing.
He'd come, driving, from fields lit like rivers,
glittering under autumnal sun.
The machete mobile clanged;
the instructor tipped (ho, bland) his spectacles.

I had not wanted
to stray
in discernment.

Can we see the air? Below, the spotted heads
in their isles of café au lait and cake—
the drifted currents, the dust electric,
sifting, divisible:
all of them gathering at the water's edge,
crying, *Sitemups! Sitemups! I'm irie!*

Each sound bite
exerted
its siphonal call.

The boar sounder swarming the Yugo,
the hero turned back to the smell that was he:
a nursed tin in frost on the window sash,
desire in the eraser of gone.
Just the swizzlestick had changed the terrain of the
ant farm. Oh nearer my god to thee.

The bird had filched
the seed
from the blue-stippled hedge.

Will we not rather, when our freedom's won
Stripe the Impala with a fiery lick
and sit out nights in the firmament
beyond the *Winkie's Watches* sign?
The hero taps the wheel with a pack of Kools.
Half-smashed. The lot of 'em.

He had the figure
to wear
one brand of grace.

Now he bats back and f---- the tetherball,
on the tar in front of the old split ranch.
Children's calls rise up from the woods below,
a caterpillar assaults the hose; a
hoodlum—no, *kid*—yanking his baggies,
crests the top of the hill.

Meeting Again, After Heine

The moon rose like a blooming flower.
The tin in the hand clattered its charge.
We walked by in the wavering hour,
I looking away, you chattering hard.

Met by luck, with like destinations,
We startled again at what ended in pique.
Strollers out, seeing us, had no notion;
A car alarm cycled its querulous shriek;

Eighth Street sank in the crack of its nightfall;
You pressed your satisfactions on me.
You in your urgency remarked *after all*
Kindling your passion was enmity;

Passion had finally erased your calm,
Made composure a prop of the past.
I mugged that street noise, din, bedlam,
Prevented my hearing your story at last.

As I walked home the strollers were thinning,
The moon bobbed above roofs like a ball,
The shade at the bus stop waved to me, beckoning,
And I nodded fast in the fast nightfall.

Sonnet of Alternate Starts for a Poem of Comparison

These people are cockroaches, a coupla cockroaches.
Those cockroaches kept the town on tenterhooks.
Like bugs, the yokels won't go away.
You cockroaches! Get thee off and how!
Whaddaya doin here, cockroaches, whaddaya say?
Without their creeping, I would have found—
A cockroach might more blameless be, you think?
O ya know daguy's a cockroach by dalook but he—
Like their namesakes, they're drawn to sludge.
Damn the cockroach life upon the lea.
What bug shall I compare with you?
You shittin me, you cockroach mouth.
Anest, the big one hies off the small.
Cockroach yer a fool off the poohbah sled.

Molloy for Girls

> To him who has nothing it is forbidden
> not to relish filth.
>
> –Samuel Beckett, *Molloy*

In the tall grass lot we sniffed the gas.
We puked jujubes. The multi-pack.

I don't know why he gave *me* rocks.
I found them in my pockets after the act.

After the act he ran across the tall grass lot
into what could have been a reservoir.

I wanted to see what jujube colors stuck
as I rolled around in the tall grass lot.

He'd've never said the words like this.
The red chunks stuck on me the best.

III

A blue broke on him from the sun,
A bullioned blue, a blue abulge. . .

Wallace Stevens, "Two Illustrations that the World
Is What You Make of It"

Run on a Warehouse

I.

What he had said came back to him.
Sectioned seat, sectioned seat.
The lift caught wind and swayed him in.
Big armoire, big armoire.

For some time he had felt it stir.
Sideboard door, sideboard door.
He sashayed through the conifers.
Dad's chair, dad's chair.

He had not known how far he'd come.
The blanket chest, the blanket chest.
A sourceless light suffused the run.
Love seat, love seat.

He had not come for his own sake.
All fixtures new, fixtures new.
Before the end he'd need to break.
Wall to wall, wall to wall.

So buckily he bore his load.
Filigreed frame, filigreed frame.
He could not see the lodge for snow.
Canopied bed, canopied bed.

He'll not forget the moment soon.
Cuckoo clock, cuckoo clock.
Now over snow a glimpse of moon.
Savvy desk, savvy desk.

There were but two things he required.
Glass breakfront, glass breakfront.
The slope was steep and he was tired.
Just a hutch, just a hutch.

II.

What heathen man there came down said
Inequity or not, there has to be
A way to bargain that there will instead
Be harbingers, or history.

How come, one said, and then one of each
Joined in finding an earnest fool
The gentleman with the counterpoint
Who could not get the present rule.

What frippery. This narrative could not
Have less to do with whim. I'm bored.
It's now that the bodice and the dots
Become the hedge for wonders scored.

Oldest Psalter

After the bath, the boxed light flickers
A lurid tale. Beyond the next hill in the streetlamp's spill
Venus clinks its goodly place.
The stratus bank doth overtake.

The comb, sprung by hair, scrapes my breast.
All the diffident noise of the dark arrest
Clamors. A cup, a dish, in the lair of the sink—
The forsythia flaps a palm, a wish—

I could not say that it was mine, before
Switching off the boxed light switch—
The postal clerk who had them stung.

I could not find the phlox, the star
To restorate the taken-over.
The sad sacked hero of the lot of them.

Poem

Green is the false nettle
and green is its bloom
and few are the tenders
you pull from your room,

fewest are the cinders
that fall from your fire,
the many times I wait at
the sparking of desire,

and full yearned, unsated
you adopt a green regret,
unfaithed a slopping kettle
you in my love, beset.

Fractured Fairy Tale

So activate then. Beforehand the birds
settle in for a roost, and the shiny clock hands
start to rattle. The frog prince bewails
his casaba schnozz. *De*-activate's more like it.

Several men rest their rakes at their crotches and begin to talk.
They are having an ur-argument. They are arguing over
pure and impure analyticity, or error theory or a nonfactualist
theory about ethics. It might be the Chinese Room Argument.
The light through the elms reminds them of dinner.
The hunger reminds them of loss.

Doze Doll Does Wiz Biz—a century that, her sleeping,
a stenotic century self-circling, noodling its tunes, drug
by the scuff of its kitchen to stand, squinting, at *thing*
coherent, drooping from clouds, bungeeing to boot.

White Exiles

Pittsburgh

"No, it's *fop*. Not sap, fop." "Yeah?—
what century you be blazing in?"
He wanked it twice, for effect.
The bugeyes flared and rolled.

Westport

It was that beverage service!
It even provided the wrong
condiments
and a truckload of calories.

Rochester

Uwanga, uwangalayma
uwanga. The red locust,
from the palm of her hand,
spun out over checkerboard turf.

Wilton

There might be a festoon with which to salve—
perhaps ministrations and some unfolding things—
that will expiate the wrecks you wrought.
What sanguine heads the tufts adorn.

Sudbury

Unguent. A nail flies softly on a cheek,
the candle sputters and then carries on.
He steered the International Travelall
through the wooded, winding roads.

Bennington

Mrs. Ainsworth clicks across the
gallery floor as the Buick pulls up
and three smelly kids run into the minimart
for all-beef sticks.

Woodstock

She was wearing the shiny gold baseball
jacket with the word *Trésor* like
handwriting across the back and leopard
spots across the lapels.

Chicago

The clutch had stuck on the Outer Drive. "Oh,
Perseph—oh dear, you do me so like shaking."
The left turn light had shorted twice. "Your
lap is where I'm pricking. Doll."

New York

So? Whine and be pissy. The abrupt
bud in the Hawaiian grove, the cheap chiseler
in the monkey suit, the filaments beneath the sill:
What made me, what I will.

Framingham

She said she thinks it was when IHOP
put turkey clubs on the menu.
Doug shovelled some sand and let it fall.
The disaster that accompanied you
to this moment made it
harder and harder to speak uh, normally.

The rapacious bags at the supermarket
were all packed tight as a drum.

Late in the evening, the stoplight at Warner
swooped in the tumbling rain.

Squish it! the children were yelling
in the garage in the light of the bulb,
and the breath that had left you came back upon you
from your perch in the far sycamore.

Landscaping for Privacy

I wanted the gigando set in this corner here,
the 36 incher under the row of cornapples
hung just as the greasy greasy grannies done.
I like to collect copper, and here it's found
beside blue hyacinth forcers, in clumps of pans.
Something's always on the stove when a visitor comes.

The kilim fans make fine lampshades for those days
when birds swarm the greening shingles lined
with that vermiculite dusting we did last week.
Repeat: your burdock dishrags will last you a life
if you sun them slowly in a makeshift pan.
The visitor should always be encouraged to eat.

Those small doilies woven from maidenhair ferns?
Just the ticket on a happ'nin' day when the crow-
house takes you hours just to rake the dung,
or thickets of linens haul slow in the wringer,
or terns pinned on the landing grouse, unsung.
Visitors are allowed to eat with their fingers.

I've filed a grievance of the nuisance brand
on the new neighbor who provided a violate view:
what once dressed eaves in honeysuckle decor
now, a dish, satellite, with camouflage crochet.
The pressings book per gingerbread's good for more.
Decorate the bluefish and the visitors stay.

Casino Night

All the matches are printed "Hook's Casino."
They do Casino Night right, here under hatches
at the Hookery Spa.

The dykes from the next bunk turned unfriendly.
I may not be cool.
Reading may not be the alternative to Hook's Casino.

Big boy! Stiffen that thought and hold it, won't you?
Yassir Igotcha, the half-Palestinian, third-Minneapolisan,
stirred at sight of the dice. I'm like nice.

But not very. I got the roil of
American swells, the bugs and the sad TV sedimentation,
the gamboling cells under glass in the stratified light,

a limpid one-two over chips on the felt.
I might not be right. Freeweights away,
Hook's wheels spin on far and long in the night.

The View from There

The old boss was surprised when you ran into her
on the street. Behind her eyelashes a model TV
hummed a sports coach and a car. The old boss
said, for instance, *Well I'm so glad things are going*
well for you with genuine surprise. She rubbed
at her eyelid and tried to revise her history of you,
invisibly. But it showed. The lazy sky and the car
gliding under the trees, the library's false front:
the view made a fit backdrop for hysteria.
She thought she was in the clear; she was wrong.

Old patrons know to patronize, a sports star told the
sports coach, although you could not hear him from
outside the store. Herr Arbeit showed me the desk by
appliances: eleven more forms to blot with dry
snow, seven mock beavers to stuff. Then show
My work is cut out to a tee.

Two Regrets

I could have shown you the way through the darkened hall.
The brass knob opened into the room with the lilacs,
the glass to the rank nursery. From each of the doorways
the boy now so bending rises and hauls now a sack.

The transom is lit with the gold from the ballroom.
Why do you hesitate on the stair to the blue gowns?
Why does the elf who attends you so carefully
look away from your pausing and frown?

I would have taken your arm at the moment you saw her
and noted the dipper that marked the dark morning.
I could have shown you the small twinkling warning and
the windows rimmed then with such green conifer.

Clock Radio

expunging Ponge

That each second escorts a fresh plash. Slatted awning, rec room wall, bald black translucence, the numerals—flip. The methodical tumbling drives it to hum at the pitch it extracts from the wires.

Its cousins in Holland sing slightly higher. Its march it propels with reluctance. Its drive is for the offbeat, the cack-handed, the apocopated. It sings with regret for its thrum.

The clock radio strives to become its grandfather only with ambivalence, spilling its pool on the nightstand with a modesty and steadiness in the clicks of its onerous job, in the particles that sworl in its wake.

Knot Me

after H.C. Westermann

The reddish glow is jacked. Ole Cliff he found
the yard out back, and it sure got the roses bright.
Criminy anchor, tippled hull, haunt of
pieces&parts in a footlocker full.

O Canada don't hold a candle to thee,
spring's air like cigar from the gunnery,
she was the slightest gal on the circuit see
and I loved her.

Yellow barn planks thrum in the hum of the
plane. Handstandin'est, sweet bargain pal,
I could have found nothing in the hickory
but what below burned frightest. Knot me.

Knit in Your Will

It was dumb luck the airline went bust
and he had to change his flight. It was
fortuitous that they were passing by
the dumpster in the dark. *It was a real break*
that the agent's steak had to cook some more.
Had you not come, I wouldn't have gone
to the acres beyond Fuller Peak.

Gentlest hull of bond, tendons that bear
to work a gait, sentiment that brought you here:
at the window in the dark, speaking tongues
that I can't hear. A bayou slush and slop
against the shore, the stiffened call of a
callou bird, the wading in a break might bear:
storm, I see the order there.

Tenderly, repeated Flo, as though she knew
the words. The gate's unstuck, and now the flock
stirs, and swarms the sky.

Chosen

Under tubed lights the blue light
pounds and pounds.
Bartleby's ghost in an assiduous swoon

pricks my buttons, three, four, six—
collars me forward, a punk at toil,
regurgitates a scrod fish bone,

—So do I! But I didn't know it had a past tense—
waves the cut, a blotto
mohel un-capped, a singing sevens without

position, listens in to *splices of my pride,*
hies Hesiod's map o faithfully,
switches offices when my back is turned.

He yells at me in Norse. Over and again
the instructional stews
confounded me. And see the brethren's back.

Earn it. What? Had he a pfennig to
call his own he'd bail.
Or rather I'd unhaunted be—I'd *haunting lack.*

Above the blue light a stippled moon creaks into place
and, in the dark,
the macro cuts a three-span wheel for a ten-palm cart,

the button bar masticulates, the wavy mind
waves off in space.
Bone collating—now *that's* a job.

Afterword *by Robert Hass*

Susan Wheeler's *Smokes* looks like a book that sets itself the task of continuous invention and surprise. The idiom is postmodern: irony, pastiche, non-sequitur, dark wit, wild shifts in diction, a funhouse falling away of narrative continuity from image to image and line to line. It doesn't exactly constitute a regnant style, but it is by now familiar enough. What makes *Smokes* such an exhilarating and unexpected performance is not the idiom, which Ms. Wheeler has down and carries off with brio, but her witty ear. It's as if she took an aspect of postmodernism, of John Ashbery's style, back through Auden to its ancestral roots in Lewis Carroll and Edward Lear and then leapt forward again to make new inventions out of it in the disoriented present.

The first stanza of the first poem in the book looks like a fairly straightforward version of this cheerfully absurd and darkly ironic style:

> The girls are drifting in their ponytails
> and their pig iron boat. So much for Sunday.
> The dodo birds are making a racket
> to beat the band. You should have come too.

So what is the faint echo you're hearing? It's the first stanza in the first poem in Robert Frost's *A Boy's Will* (1915):

> I'm going out to clean the pasture spring;
> I'll only stop to rake the leaves away
> (And wait to watch the water clear, I may);
> I shan't be gone long.—You come too.

This doesn't just parody Frost. It's in fact a kind of homage, and it sets the two conditions of poetry at the beginning and the end of the century next to one another with a kind of pure glee. This effect occurs over and over in *Smokes*; sometimes Wheeler uses quotation as here, and sometimes she accomplishes it with sheer music, pastiches of sound quarried, as in Auden and Lewis Carroll, from the whole repertoire of English poetry. It's very surprising. It's like listening to the still chancy and experimental transmission of the postmodern vehicle gleefully downshifting into the breezy updrafts of the traditional musics of English verse, and then lurching into the future again.

Here is the second half of the sonnet she calls "Beavis' Day Off:"

> How long could he crimp the diesel in the dark?
> The bedlam was breathing its own air now;
> the parrot shivering in the freezer glared at the hen.

The assured craziness is what we come to expect of her, though writing as firm as that second line is one of the things that sets Wheeler apart. The reader anticipates a jump cut and gets one in the next two lines:

> *Please it's time* said Meg. And each infernal
> truism struck a package deal with tin.

Fair enough, but listen to the last lines. First she gives us a loopy pastiche of an early poem of Pound's—"Blandula, Tenulla, Vagula" of 1911—and then a final two lines of unexpectedly gorgeous and pure music in a ballad measure, the last line giving the whole a purity like blues:

> What hast thou, O nut job, with paradise?
> The sparks O they crested the floor then they floated
> and she lay down on fine braids and she cried.

A few of the poems, like "Shanked on the Red Bed," spill over into the pure anapests of Victorian nonsense verse:

> The century was breaking and the blame was on default,
> The smallest mammal redolent of what was in the vault,
> The screeches shrill, the ink-lines full of interbred regret—
> When I walked out to look for you the toad had left his net.

There are Skeltonics here from the meters of 16th century poetry, riffs that sound like the measures of A.E. Housman—

Green is the false nettle
and green is its bloom
and few are the tenders
you pull from your room

—homages to Samuel Beckett—one of the poems is called "Molloy for Girls"— and send-ups of the prose poetry of Francis Ponge.

Smokes contains elegies, poems of urban and domestic angst, laments, invectives, cakewalks, struts. It's very much of the moment but it is also a deeply literary book—how could it not be? And its confident, rueful, and playful grasp of its tradition is eye-opening and, sardonic as it is, boisterous fun.

Author's Notes

The line, "Will we not rather, when our freedom's won," in "The Blanching Heart" is excerpted from Ezra Pound's "Blandula, Tenella, Vagula," and "What hast thou..." in "Beavis' Day Off," paraphrases the same Pound poem's "What hast thou, O my soul, with paradise?" The quotations in "The Lip of the Snow in Lapland" are Corinthians 12:8-11. "Fractured Fairy Tale" uses remarks of the philosopher Paul Boghossian. In "The Dogwood and the The," "Summer bun it drive me crazy" manhandles "Summer bunnies drive me crazy," from R. Kelly's single "Summer Bunnies" and "Cool summa, wahm in the winta," advice on raising children given to Carrie in the film version of Theodore Dreiser's *Sister Carrie*. The child Norton ("Exemplification Avenue") in Flannery O'Connor's story, "The Lame Shall Enter First," hanged himself under the attic peak, and Helga loses her wooden leg to a Bible salesman ("You Should Know: Invective") in O'Connor's "Good Country People." "Song for the Spirit of Natalie Going" borrows some language (in English translation) from Stéphane Mallarmé's "A Tomb for Anatole." In "Chosen," "a three-span wheel for a ten-palm cart" is from Hesiod's *Works and Days*, and John Berryman's *Dream Songs* was the source for "bone collating" (30) and "splices of his pride" (166). Several brief phrases in "Smokes" come from James Schuyler's "Hymn to Life."

SUSAN WHEELER is on the faculty of the MFA program in creative writing at The New School for Social Research in New York City. She has been the recipient of a Pushcart Prize and of two fellowships from the New York Foundation for the Arts. Her first collection, *Bag 'o' Diamonds*, was chosen by James Tate to receive the Norma Farber First Book Award from the Poetry Society of America, and was shortlisted for the Los Angeles Times Book Award in Poetry. She lives in New York City.